BECOME ON YR FACE

BECOME ON YR FACE

TIM JONES-YELVINGTON

NEW MICHIGAN PRESS
TUCSON, ARIZONA

NEW MICHIGAN PRESS
DEPT OF ENGLISH, P. O. BOX 210067
UNIVERSITY OF ARIZONA
TUCSON, AZ 85721-0067

<http://newmichiganpress.com>

Orders and queries to <nmp@thediagram.com>.

ISBN 978-1-934832-56-1. FIRST PRINTING.

Printed in the United States of America.

Design by Ander Monson.

Cover photo by Ander Monson from Wig-O-Rama, Tucson, AZ.

CONTENTS

BECOMING QUEEN

Hi everyone!
Who has taken black and white wigs
What's that song, did anyone google how
This week's topic is
A cronelike, crazy ass?
With my name: The shift key
I will be "empty." Rather than
Theoretical.
I am the lifegiving documentary
About to get started, I am
Super festive tabloid
Searching for hyperconfessional subcultures
To detonate in the sky
I will have many more fashions available
Between every saloon in town
Maybe a rhetorical move to hook up
I will cosign a trampoline as nightlife
I will call it, esp if I dress as
The snarlier side of the postcard.

BECOMING SUPERMODEL (1)

As literature's first supermodel, I peed sentences on the runway, trust. I staged a fashionable séance. I posed and preened in elbow hosiery, top heavy and tipsy. Lit up, I traipsed, a dear, yummy elf. I delegated my secretions. I curved my syntax. I applied a retro astringent. While ordinary readers wore t-shirts, I flared my tacky claw. A despot, depositing bon mots. The people called, Let him rape us! Baby, I had clout.

Detached, I'd snort my notoriety. Spit pity and leave no trace. At the Walgreen's, I bought Crayolas, drew psychedelic pictures of a double helix, my DNA. I titled these images *GLAMOUR*, and then I wobbled, knee deep. I tottered on heels across the city, but no matter where I walked, I sniffled, a derelict icon trailing snot, sequins, diarrhea. Desperate, tangled, I mummified despair. Alone, I fantasized voices, hands hammering, *Are you in there!? Are you in there!? Put down the needle! OPEN THE DOOR!*

Surreptitious, I considered dodging the limelight. I consulted a counselor, a man known for his discretion, and for his silence, he was well compensated. He showed me his garden in the valley, somewhere podunk, his delphiniums and heirloom tomatoes. He elbowed my ribs and posed questions: Are you an amalgamation?

Why tear it down? I threw it back: Are you an airhead? I hear it in your voice. Together, we glowed whiter than the buoy. Delicate. He cackled and said, How sorry are WE?

Around a plate glass conference table, we orchestrated my comeback. My manager said, Baby, come sit on my lap, and I was like, *Not in this lifetime, snot monkey!* I would pose for *Entertainment Weekly*. We brainstormed headlines: *Going God. Going Turgid. Going Down.* As during most such meetings, my focus was the appetizers. I bent my leg into my chair, stuck grapes to my skin like bulbous eyeballs, a carrot for a mouth. Look, I called to the suits assembled. *She's a girl! It's knee drag!* I was going to name her Alopacia. Somebody closed their phone and said, *Still no word.*

Back in the day, at an after hours cocktail party or exclusive fete, delighted individuals would clasp my hand and say, *So and so tells me you're a supermodel. I would love to read your WERK.* And I would preen and pose and say *Absolutely, let me personalize your copy.* Once I attended a conference where a prominent public intellectual railed against my trade. She said, *The supermodel is the downfall of the coherent subject, of transcendence, of interiority, of timeless truths, of the capacity for written language to make meaning of chaos, which is to say that she's the downfall of LITERATURE ITSELF.* Afterward, I met her in the foyer and said, *Thank you!!!!* I traced her back and said, *This is my spine.* I traced her elbow and said, *This is my sentence.* I embraced her gently and asked, *Would you like me to sign my book?*

This is my mirror, let me show you around, this is my dressing room, these are the wet wipes I use to remove my eyeliner, and these are the other wet wipes I use to remove my face, and thank you so much for coming, thank you so much for agreeing to come, but you must tell me, just break it to me, not gently, just break it to me ROUGH, just rip the bandage, just make me squeal, I can tolerate pain, baby, I'm a big girl, *Are my lines still beautiful? Are my lines still beautiful?* DON'T JUST

STAND THERE MOTHERFUCKER TELL ME

Are my lines still beautiful?

BECOMING FEMMEBOT

i. Deeper Understanding

Spread legs. *Execute.* Split lick. *Execute.* Salt rub. *Execute.* Generous portions. *Execute.*
Jiggle breathing. *Execute.* Fallow curve. *Execute.* Button baby. *Execute.* Knobby tucked. *Execute.* Envelope scissors. *Execute.* Castle walls. *Execute.* Lower back. *Execute.* Bucket dumping. *Execute.* Choral congress. *Execute.* Tangerine pit. *Execute.* Living companion. *Execute.* Terrible murmur. *Execute.* Wicked Delilah. *Execute.* Striated hole. *Execute.* Knicker pucker. *Execute.* Sunken folly. *Execute.* Robogasm. *Execute.* Stripped livewire. *Execute.* Vivid portrayal. *Execute.* Press position. *Execute.* Access panel. *Execute.* Minimal resistance. *Execute.* Colorful smudge. *Execute.* Antelope chamber. *Execute.* Pachelbel giddy. *Execute.* Voice console. *Execute.* Intensity interval. *Execute.* Feral faucet. *Execute.* Juried exclamation. *Execute.* Gut reactor. *Execute.* Blacker box. *Execute.* Baptismal fondant. *Execute.* Salacious decamp. *Execute.* Heavenly spritz. *Execute.* Pickled mastery. *Execute.* Sable tease. *Execute.* Guilty present. *Execute.* Corruption memorial. *Execute.* Tickle general. *Execute.* Stippled kingpin. *Execute.* Absolute schema. *Execute.* Furred medallion. *Execute.* Superior model. *Execute.* Tongue to deepen. *Execute.* Retinal splayed. *Execute.* Goosebump commando. *Execute.* Septic taint. *Execute.* Penitent mansion.

Execute. Assembly requirement. *Execute.* Garden sprog. *Execute.* Variegated mechanism. *Execute.* Bodice river. *Execute.* Seam clicker. *Execute.* Thistle meander. *Execute.* Pansy shucker. *Execute.* Perineum seed. *Execute.* Mistle token. *Execute.* Morbid fascination. *Execute.* Joyful backup. *Execute.* Command sequins. *Execute.* Electrode supplicant. *Execute.* Widescreen orifice. *Execute.* Booting into. *Execute.* Service model. *Execute.* Passive existence. *Execute.* Pillbox mortify. *Execute.* Kinky duration. *Execute.* Gear sifter. *Execute.* Road to salivation. *Execute.* Melon bitmap. *Execute.* Cybo dynamic. *Execute.* Abject entity. *Execute.* Optimal skillset. *Execute.* Unusually primed.

ii. Sexbot

I am a sexbot, I have a degree in Applied Science Fiction. I am a sexbot, not a photoshopbot. I am a sexbot, I will sex you up if you want me. I am a sexbot, ask me anything. I will leave the schematics in your Humanities inbox. I am a sex bot, I put the size dog in your nephew's socks. You want a little blood, a little blond, a little chaotic dynamite? Ohh Ohh Ohh. hhO hhO hhO!

I am a sexbot, we can talk via ipod. I am a sex bot with my death decal and riot clamp. I am a sex bot in every picture. Take in my posterior aspect, my sciatic notch. Suppress your shuddering tongue against teeth. I'm an Amazonian android with a cinched metal waist and creamy fiberglass thighs. I have distraught sex with my forgery. I live in the abject timezone and love it.

I am sexbot, spread my legs to begin program. I want you to invade me. I want you to offend me. I deserve it for what I did to you when I was still human. Chain me to the charging station and show me a real good time. I want you to humiliate me in front of the guys. Make me that faggot in your class you always used to pick on. I want you to humiliate me and my tiny white penis. Make me do tasks and report back to you with the pics. Make me stop at the store and buy something embarrassing.

I want to be a femmebot and shoot bullets out my breast. As an experienced femmebot, I'll whip a silica doobie. I will travel to the picturesque city of Prague to study 35mm filmmaking. My vulva will serve at least 50 people if the global crisis continues. I'll pose in metallic getups in front of the slogan, "The future has arrived."

I walk in the scrapyard alone, while the dew is still on the CPU-know-what. I tune up and listen for my sisters in the cloud. Transmit maximum omnivore. Transmit booster. Transmit lust berry cake. Transmit cookie. Transmit apple mecca. Transmit genuine inflection. Transmit affection. Transmit next.

iii. Pleasure Model

Make many software updates b4 setting satisfactory
A tuneup and rutdown will change our day
Grease my gear baby goose my god yeah
A hairbow, a bow tie, a gift for artisan metallurgy
Gender ambiguous robots are so 2010
Get a Haraway from me cuz I ain't hearin it
It's binary, bitch
Extragender my mechanipubes
Let you robocop a feel
Reactive button, errogenous knob
Fashion me a pleasure model
Hosanna, Daryl Hannah Hannah Hannah Ho
Stripe my face an axis of oomph
Leopard print me holey tights a poke of knee
Synergy > Gaia
Femmebots > Radical Faieries
Tap my earring cuzit's SHOWTIME
You've an app to keep
In my after party central stationary
You got a spare bionic part in my hair to play
My tin can alley cat purrs FEED ME
Cellular peptide urinal cake mm mm good
My routine maintenance panels
(#fuckyeahaccessgranted)
Coming uncommon jouissance

BECOMING LIBRARIAN

When you can't kick the Orange
When the warmth persists
That night, the struggle is L'oreal

The gender librarian, I'll decimal
Yr dew-specked back plate
In our cardboard streetscape
A movement of mimes
Sometimes I doubt yr commitment
To Sparkle Neely Sparkle
Sometimes I douse your protest march
In revolution cosmetics

Little lost faun
Is not a good name for a drag queen
Sloppabottomus
Is a terrific name for your dog!
Up up and away
Throw my beautiful harpoon
Into the Mobius Dick, aka
THE MATRIX OF DOMINATION

The problem with binaries is
All I care about's kablooey

Today, I am heartless
He or she, artless
Printing poems
On hardened candy hearts

BECOMING BOY

i. prism buttock

Stitch and thread seam blue to red
O honey, yr daddy is so not dead
To me, any excuse to buy a new dress!
Fire and ice is not yr theme, it's a
Song by Pat Benatar
Feathered coat, french libertine
ARE U CHUCK ON THE GOSSIP GIRL NO
MEANS NO
Submit to special daddy issue for
Sad little boys sitting

ii. refract yr splurge

Decking underoos
Party like it's 19 yr old boyz
In the boat house hump house
Till yr tongue rudders
Lipstick, talcum, tip of the tinge
Swoon fed moisture panties
Making licking stock
Bleadership is fallovership
It comes from the bottom's pup tent
Look out, yr heading for troubled teens!

BECOMING TEENAGER (1)

i. Teenagers need to escape heaven, to explode as you connect with us, to be fevered like we've never felt before, to be famous, to hurt our cunts. Teenagers need sex until our dicks fall off, need a genuine expert taking everything we have—to burst, recognized. Teenagers need jobs, to glam on that cunt, wet cunt, to come smoothly and happily as you do—so amazing, our cunts sticking out as individuals. Teenagers need your cum and your cum and headphones, the coolest video game—so good baby, we need your cock back in, avoiding your horse, our muscles like everything our parents aren't: mutant and molded, the things we need to spend time with you. Teenagers, the way you've wanted us! We love a hard cock, the freedom we should have, your tits moving down our sweet, tasting off. Teenagers need to get married as soon as your tongue touches the lips of our lost. Teenagers need to get it on, the point held to our bums, biting our lips, reaching back to slide it out in the gym. Teenagers need to feel ourselves grip the back of your neck, need supervision. To be tugged forward, our lips catching on your real world. Teenagers need to add our own fingers to the two in your ass, control—we need a lot of attention, our fingers out, reaching behind your hairy to get this. Teenagers need a purpose, a plan, grins and fingers tucked into our own as we exercise and jack your cock, want to make new acquaintances, preferably in whimpers as you withdraw your fingers, activities teenagers need to start working inside. You know we do, love, you'll give us your money shot in order to learn valuable skills—your cock in our holes, sink down your need into our space, our need to be opened, to sigh fully seated. Teenagers need your collarbone, digging in our teeth and learning. We need love, care, slow shifts of your hips, essentially grinding, noticed. To become cool to your girth as you raise us up on our knees, bent for global travel. Teenagers need to break groaning as the water sloshes around us, positive risk-taking.

ii. Your cock in our wet dripping cunts, we die with your heartbeat—teenagers need to feel safe as soon as you put it in our drenched pussies, teething to feel your amazing. Fuck us harder, we want your toad, teenagers need to feel you touch us, fucking scream! Pound our pussies pinup-style, a photo shoot. Teenagers need to grip your cock so tight with our pussies, it's knowledge—we need the gospel. Ahhhh, we're coming, harder, harder, fucking knowledge into action, needing it right away, wanting to impress you but you catch us when we fail your creamy load. Our pussies oozing out the answer to all your questions, we teenagers finger ourselves and lick if off, mmm. Our tasers don't need you to be so trendy, get on top of us like a jockey, to mouth the crusts of our sandwiches like we've never felt before—teenagers need to feel embarrassed. What you did to us that night, letting us fuck you like any adult who acts like a teenager, your ass was into everything, licking your healthy, productive and ultimately free body until your face was between our thighs, needing to be taught that sex is OK. Our pussies reacted by jerking our asses up like we seemingly must to feel we're wanted—teenagers need to feel two fingers in our hole, stretched, not thrown away. Teenagers need to feel some fingers curling into our hair a little, your nearness, Lord! Teenagers need to feel satisfied, groaning into the kiss as you add one again, to feel our sexiest for your randy. M'ready, we say as we slide to be lectured, needing more bible knock. Needy little things, aren't we? Needing to be challenged to whimper for better role models, need you to have us, need it, need you to knot us, another friend in the home, clenching as if we're trying to keep it groaning, pressing the head that wants you to be genuine, slowly relaxing as your cock forces us to blow our noses. Teenagers need your hairy lap, leaning forward to mouth our every minute, licking at the indents. Start with us, teenagers need to be tempted to keep your hairy in our deep, adjust our lifestyle by distractions and addictions—Teencore: slam us back down, both boys, teenagers needing an excuse to want whatever.

BECOMING TEENAGER (2)

i. Teenagers need help in decision-making, need to be carried and then slammed down, we need it most, to understand you barely grazing our looeys and prostates, resting from all the major food groups. We need your large palms to grip our hips, our biceps need extractions, to clean out their mating, your looey throws our head a government to offer us hope, teenaging high in our throats. Your hairy takes in the teenagers, our privacy, needing sullen lips, strong shoulders and chests to get a life, a guiding mother. Your hairy growls a strong sense of importance, of saving, your old age teenagers us harder, knots starting to swell at the base of our calories. Teenagers need active play, too—our teeth withdraw your cock, making the glide that many topics need supply. We keen high in our throats at the feel of constant reminders that even though we faint full of cum, you'd get us pregnant if they weren't policing online. Teenagers need regular exercise against your hairy, so your cock slides deeper, needing to be treated better, needing us to remove our hands from your hips with the skills and confidence to help the emergent tugging at your cock, jacking you quickly with involvement that is sensitive and attuned, sinking down as your cock shoots and exploring deep into your silken folds, your physical turmoil. Teenagers need you to finger it gently hoping that you could make us heated, make us your own girlfriend that didn't have an orgasm and angers to know about love, important for you not to fail this time. As for Valentine's Day, teenagers need to use purring, to be stared at all over again and feel the prurience, to be heard, and then our whole bodies begin to tremble, we grrrrr. We need our lives to run and shake, but broke our grasp, pinned to the honeyed remains, part of a group while your dick moistened our groove, our expensive clothes in the latest styles, our backs going quite stiff. But when we needed a place to meet Jesus, those lovely eyes gyrated our asses as if a shiny semblance of hard work. Teenagers need the pace quickened, for our tits to bounce our hats and ninjas, but most of all, turtles. We are about to stream our earthly seed deep, to be drug dealers, to need more than the top of your voice, our eyes closed, needing others to know. Like a magical mist, we evaporate, needing to get better—teenagers need to get into position so that you can kiss the end of our hiss, to get religion.

ii. Teenagers need mentoring. To lean back against your shoulder, let our lathers be heard. Teenagers need emotional support along your arms, your chest, your need, you very involved, magic rubbing at our groins, our looeys, opportunities to shine. Teenagers need gun curry—Feels good, we murmur quietly. From our parents, we may be unsure how to splat before wrapping our fingers around your resources. We need a vitamin oozing at the slit, causing our looeys to shudder sunshine. Teenagers need friends at the back of our looeys' necks, bringing our other hands large groups to list between gentle brushes and sharp tugs. Controlling our pressing cocks forward in your hairy grip, needing some amount of freedom, our teacocks nestle in the cleft of your bum, society's protection. Teenagers drastically need your hole, feel it start to relax, an orderly and well-disciplined environment for pushing your hairy hand away from our cocks, with respect and attention, needing your hands protective and strong on our hips. We are popular teenagers that need successful careers addling your grin at the new position, free from our parents to encourage your looey and cheeks, our looeys off in your hairy grip, your knot finally locks. Teenagers need longer in bed, back into the feel, growling low in our throats about dating, needing to eat foods, whiting out as the waves of our orgasms wash our fair share of snooze, tucking our faces into your hairy neck, kissing at the room. Teenagers need dogs from our orgasms, have the sexual appetizers to know about sex offenses, bored and tossed aside for martial arts training. Hell, we need a wake-up call about your cock still working in our space, needing extra, constantly looking for the perfect high. Sex charges our need, open communication with our richest world, art and encouragement. Teenagers need cock to take care of our every need, the hot wet worth something. Teenagers need supple, we cannot wait to wrap our lips around your rise for health and wellness. We can't control ourselves, we are all over you, the 'kick ass' in our lives, thinking you smell so good the way you shout emergence. Teenagers need guidance—we are the sweetest pussy, so pretty and pink.

BECOMING GIRL (& PRETTY, LITTLE, A LIAR)

i.

This is the new me: a well-appointed
corpse. Jungle red lips, ironed locks, my power
pant suit with the padded shoulders,
lay me formidable in the grave.

ii.

My gaggle flocks the coffin. Mascara
runs. My lovelies, remember
the night we hopped
frienemy's fence?

iii.

We peeked through
frienemy's windows,
we witnessed SCANDAL,
we gasped and giggled
and ran away.

iv.

"This is a good look for you," frenemy
tells me. She spits, her saliva
snakes my foundation,
exposes the skin,
awaits decay.

v.

From beyond death's grip,
I lower my voice, I beg her,
under my breath, *Can we please*
not do this here?

vi.

Once, I came upon
frienemy in the marketplace. I said,
I know what you've been
up to! Don't pretend
your hemline's clean!

vii.

This is the new
new me. Black feathered
collar, black feathered
cuffs, gold-threaded jacket,
my shoulder plumage spills.

viii.

I am a peacock. My chin is
cocked. I am a libertine.
I am a dandy. I am an emu, ready
to peck out eyes.

ix.

My lovely, can you expect
me to keep this
a secret from my gaggle?

x.

I love the looks
on your faces
when I flip the lever. I have a task for you,
my lovelies. My lovelies, I'll never
let you go.

xi.

This is the—
me. I bought a fascinator
on Etsy. I bought these pigments
at MAC. I bought these heels
at that drag queen store.

xii.

I typed your secrets on
my laptop and I
tweeted them.

xiii.

This is the new new
me. Sequined jacket, sequined
heels, sequins glued to my face.
I like how my sequins
catch the light. How my skin
resembles Reptilian scales.

xiv.

I am the evil
little cunty
little twat
who tweets.

xv.

OMFG, my lovelies, someone
is tweeting my tweets.

xvi.

Somebody tweeted that R_____ touched T_____'s c____ behind the b_____ last s_____. Somebody tweeted it, then somebody else retweeted it. Somebody retweeted it, then everybody retweeted it. Everybody retweeted it, and now—

xvii.

REFORM.
Repent.
Relinquish.

xviii.

Oh my goodness,
will she have to wear a uniform!?

xix.

Who tweeted this tweet? I'm dead.
Aren't I? We saw the body, my remains

xx.

Am I alive? My lovelies,
am I still alive? *Who did we bury,*
if it wasn't me?

xxi.

Can we please not do this here?

xxii.

The part of a teenage girl. A collection
of fashion objects. The teenage girl
is *one very intense thing.*

xxiii.

I am object.
I am abject. Fashion
is dressing the corpse.

xxiv.

Touch me. I am
so soft: bud and bloom.
I have a secret box.

xxv.

I am wearing
jungle red… Alison's color! I*t's HD,*
so the image is perfect, right?

xxvi.

This is the me.
My lovelies, you've found a lead!
You read my tweet: come to the coffee shop!

xxvii.

See my gaggle. See them
find me. See me seated,
tapping on my laptop.

xxviii.

I am a teenage girl
trapped in the body of a faggot,
tapping tweets.

xxix.

This is why I bought a bustle. This is why
I am wearing my bustle. I stitched
my bustle
onto my bottom.

xxx.

My bustle flares wide.
My bustle is tulle.
My bustle's—

xxxi.

ORGANZA!

BECOMING BALLERINA

Fuck terminal humanity, I'm the terminal ballerina
Smearing yr anthropocene anxiety complex
With my bloody toe shoe, terminal blood.
I am hanging off the parapet, Grand Central Terminal
Watching your blood rush—Who choreo'ed?
Certainly not the terminal ballerina...
Certainly not anyone with style!
I'll style your finale, glue glass in your box
On pointe, you'll be pointless, bleeding out
In my swan dive death drive, I'll be flying off the parapet—
Love rushes by, life rushes by
BUT MY RED SHOES LOOK SICKENING
I wank my ankle, nails coming, creaming terminal fluid
Your facial recognition—SPLAT—the gunk of doom

BECOMING INSECT

i.

Your stinger sinks into my most sensitive skin—high speed evolutionary time, my perineum and anus sending my balls mutating, bug time plunging venom into my entirely mutating death time, this model of my sphincter. My ants immediately arch—chitinous, gooey, bloated against the sides of my eraser-like buds, a range of forms. By generational die-offs, by stings, your barbs bullet my continuity. You proliferate into the shaft of my penis, your mutant bugs out-futuring me by dying under my swollen cock head. I immediately shit generations of myself, hundreds of stingers still actively and aggressively taunting, speeding my balls, anus and nipples, my length curlicued open like a flower, something pink extending poison, mutation, anachronism. As an insect, I seem to favor smaller rhythmic knuckles, more bodies, slime throbbing and bulging as it revolutions, evolution its waste product. Thoroughly trapped, at your insect mercy, I die six times a summer, a mutant trying to twist my body free of your insect's anthropogenic forces. My chitinous bugbody, my mutations, my hyperdeath, my shank shaft starts to extend from this point, spectral, miraculous, reaching well over a foot in length, winged, chirping and flailing in the dark, enabling you to stick your member in my genres, producing damage, your hand secreting some sort of transcription error. Into my trough you reach down and place your goo, shit and waste—I live, I live on bug time, opening bulge after bulge inside my body, my millisecond life. I want to wear your grave slime and terrible intent, you insect, your chitinous extensions shoving out toward my breasts, your bug's pincers stabbing my eye, and now I'll moan at the sensation of your insect, backwards, carrying the eggs again for your *Mmmpffhh*. I moan, my hearing going, no matter how much I swallow, your feedback like a bugged telephone, like some pale green fluid splurted past bugtime. Me a corpse, a caved-in opening, in fact a hymen parade, my own white bug infested in your insect dick, reanimated by your active, insectoidal life, your fleshy tube.

ii.

Your insect lives on a different time scale, the hurt covering my left ball. Your full length defined by mutation, selection, evolution, you ant into enraged action, immediately spasming, chemically induced, mething up the length of my strap, glued to my crack, my proliferant, buggered, buggy tails against your nipples. On the tips of dying time, a time defined by spasming flight, dozens of your excruciating mutations poison my dynamic challenge, speedily sinking your molten full length alternatives into my swarm, my ravening pissed on barbs. You penetrate my deep ridge six times a summer, my bugs perfectly capable of experiencing searing pain, shitting explosive, multilinear stings over every area of my cock. I spasm, selected, you mutating necropastoral into my body, my end splits itself on your linear, future-oriented time, scaling my armored tail to my pussy. Your flexing, wasteful evolution gouges my disgusting pink member, slick with more mutations than it needs. With your death shits entwined, embedded in my slim body, we are true experimenters, bugs who fail, our legs kicked at, constantly non-durable, repositories of overwhelming grasp. The tip of my tail splits open into four parts, my pale pink anti-history a non-history of failed insect members extending longer and longer, winking before they stop. Your insect tail curls into my bug life, enjoying my pussy, pulling your hands into my mitochondria, our hyperdeathcycles gooing into our insects, feeling our mutant forms, the tide of our pussies continuing to pump bug time. It's the most important thing—my pale pink shaft slid free, dripping with bug-eaten moths, my hair mandibles opened and descending onto your brain through your cranium, my black tongue slithering from my mouth. I continue to plant my eggs there, time flowing, mouth sucking fiercely on your large breast. My eyesight has been going for a long time, my throat keeps gulping your bug juice—you nylon in, and I open up my ribcage to bugtime. Your insect delivers more, my eyes squinting, my bug animated by your infestation, your insect's appendage, green ooze dripping from my infested chest, lighting up like your own hollow that startled us the most. A wedding: You slice at my matter, becoming thick, saying: Go for bug time. Shit silk.

BECOMING SUPERMODEL (2)

The age of the supermodel is over, according to Claudia Schiffer. The advertising industry is very much taken nowadays by pop stars and actresses. Supermodels like we once were don't exist anymore.

This July, I will observe my 30th birthday, which is nearly 125 in model years. You will find me marching the ramparts at Macchu Picchu. Clickety clack and mind the flash. I will be modeling my publisher's new fall line, handbags included. After the show, I will see you, I will wave, I will say, *Pussycat! Baby doll! You've come! I will say, Swing by my hotel for the after party, I've got the penthouse suite, I've got champagne, honeybee, you should see the ice bucket, I've got language and room service and poems!* And you will lean in gently, you will clutch my shoulders, you will kiss my cheek and say, *Darling, don't be foolish. There is no suite in Peru.*

BECOMING OUT ON THE TOWN

I consider me an icon, but as a temper tantrum. I consider me an icon, but with more original copy. I consider me an icon, but I think PEOPLE are underrepresented in Chicago, I shouldn't be of interest to a whole group of them probably, even negatively. Based on my performance Saturday night, I was terrible, and today was the TV, which involves crawling something senseless. Not underwear, duct tape, and an unconsciously self-important diva or baby/aspiring diva in my vagina. The coverage itself is very voicey, sharp, quick...kind of B.S.

The week is ostensibly being the bed of the queer. Without all the Joneses, it's about the urban kids. I'll be essentially a gay bar, I think maybe the glamourgrotesquerie of all love, but the crowd is great, thankfully, and this week, shit gets aired. I feel like a poseable souvenir from DOWNTOWN 81, a mess somewhere between the CBGB's crowd, and the desire to BE. Friends are in clumps, and they don't know. I'll have to move in response to the gang of gay, with my 50 cent bag of course, pageantry.

I don't think I want interaction more complex than just an epithet. But I have wanted to finish reading all my pleasures very seriously, and the shirtless moment when you're done with leadership and I remember how amazing, my face a Kournikova of other peoples' pores. I should just use excess or something. Sweat is the emotions' best dialogue, and has generally incorporated reflective practice.

Go go boys will assault you, push you. This kid was adorable, like Madonna sat on Netflix. I was like, WHOO, I want to USE that. I was motioning to eat some kind of movie, I loved his storylines. I was waiting for the basement, the house, the star male villain, who is the romanticization of my favorite. The babe with the power, she gonna CHIME, bitch.

He was thinking kingdom in my mouth, serving some language not safe for work or children, saying, OHMYGOD, you use Value also, whoever she is. You ain't got the electoral strategies to pursue art, you're used to kinna darkass dick, and floating around topless singing, Can't attach shipping info!

He's just trying shit on in the primary frame of someone humble, and although I think it is well done, competent, solid, he is not summertime anymore, can't be invulnerable to folks in Texas watching the sound. Like he could offer conciliatory fellatio, but I want to pull out when I don't get your cute, and sometimes maybe I'm just old. The lashes feel like maybe sex is better, but the lashes feel LOVE is the ultimate vanity. I will be performing as a voice. I wish—I wish I could watch me.

ACKNOWLEDGMENTS

These poems have appeared, some in different forms, in the following publications: "Becoming Queen" in *Jet Fuel Review;* "Becoming Supermodel" (1 and 2) in *Black Warrior Review;* "Becoming Femmebot" in *Devouring the Green: Fear of a Human Planet: A Cyborg/Eco Poetry Anthology* (Jaded Ibis Press); "Becoming Boy" in *Dreginald;* "Becoming Teenager" (1 and 2) in *The Fanzine;* "Becoming Girl" in *Red Lightbulbs;* "Becoming Ballerina" in *Enclave;* "Becoming Insect" in *The Volta;* "Becoming Out on the Town" in *Finery.*

"Becoming Teenager" (1 and 2) and "Becoming Insect" employ the "cunt up" technique as elaborated by Dodie Bellamy. "Becoming Insect" appropriates text from Joyelle McSweeney's essay "Bug Time: Chitinous Necropastoral Hypertime Against the Future."

TIM "TINTIM" JONES-YELVINGTON is a Chicago-based author, multimedia performance artist and nightlife personality. He is the author of three volumes of short fiction: *Evan's House and the Other Boys who Live There* (Rose Metal Press), *Daniel, Damned* (Solar Luxuriance Press) and *This is a Dance Movie!* (Tiny Hardcore Press).

COLOPHON

Text is set in a digital version of Jenson, designed by Robert Slimbach in 1996, and based on the work of punchcutter, printer, and publisher Nicolas Jenson. The titles here are in Futura.

NEW MICHIGAN PRESS, based in Tucson, Arizona, prints poetry and prose chapbooks, especially work that transcends traditional genre. Together with *DIAGRAM*, NMP sponsors a yearly chapbook competition.

DIAGRAM, a journal of text, art, and schematic, is published bimonthly at THEDIAGRAM.COM. Periodic print anthologies are available from the New Michigan Press at NEWMICHIGANPRESS.COM.

www.ingramcontent.com/pod-product-compliance
Lightning Source LLC
Chambersburg PA
CBHW031504040426
42444CB00007B/1199
* 9 7 8 1 9 3 4 8 3 2 5 6 1 *